HEALTHY SEAS

by Carol Inskipp

A⁺

Smart Apple Media

First published in 2006 by Evans Brothers Limited
2A Portman Mansions, Chiltern Street, London W1U 6NR

Produced for Evans Brothers Limited by White-Thomson Publishing Ltd.
210 High Street, Lewes, East Sussex BN7 2NH

Editorial: Catherine Clarke; Design: Tinstar Design Ltd.; Consultant: Ed Green;
WWF Reviewers: Patricia Kendell and Cherry Duggan; Picture Research: Amy Sparks

Acknowledgements
Corbis **pp. 7** (Robert Holmes), **17** (Wolfgang Kaehler), **20** (Yann Arthus-Bertrand), **26** (Jay Dickman) **33** (right) (Natalie Fobes), **39** (Amos Nachoum), **42**, **43** (Martin Jones); Ecoscene **pp. 8** (Reinhard Dirscherl), **11**, **22** (Robert Nichol), **23** (Visual&Written), **25** (Robert Baldwin), **36**; ICRAN (Mike MaCoy) **p. 41**; Marine Stewardship Council (logo) **p. 33** (left); OSF Ltd Photo Library **pp. 5** (Japack Photo Library), **6** (Peter Cook), **9** (Daniel Cox), **10** (Index Stock Imagery), **12** (David Fleetham), **13** (Pacific Stock), **14**, **16** (Ben Osborne), **19** (bottom) (Howard Hall), **19** (top) (David Tipling), **21** (Jon Arnold Images), **24** (Index Stock Imagery), **27** (Animals Animals/Earth Scenes), **28** (Index Stock Imagery), **29** (Robert Harding Picture Library Ltd.), **30** (Keith Ringland), **32** (Index Stock Imagery), **34** (Gerard Soury), **35** (Index Stock Imagery), **37** (Index Stock Imagery), **38** (Pacific Stock), **45** (Pacific Stock); Scottish Quality Salmon (www.scotishsalmon.co.uk) **p. 31**; Topfoto (IPA Harold Chapman) **p. 44**.

Cover photograph reproduced with permission of Pacific Stock/OSF/Photolibrary.

World Wildlife Fund-UK Registered Charity No. 1081247. A company limited by guarantee number 4016725.
Panda symbol © 1986 WWF. ® WWF Registered trademark.

Published in the United States by Smart Apple Media
2140 Howard Drive West, North Mankato, Minnesota 56003

Library of Congress Cataloging-in-Publication Data

Inskipp, Carol, 1948-
Healthy seas / by Carol Inskipp.
p. cm. — (Sustainable futures)
ISBN-13: 978-1-58340-980-0
1. Marine ecology—Juvenile literature. 2. Endangered ecosystems—Juvenile literature.
I. Title. II. Voices

QH541.5.S3I543 2006
577.7'27—dc22   2005057613

9 8 7 6 5 4 3 2 1

Contents

Why are healthy seas important?

"Sustainability" is a word meaning "the ability to continue to support itself indefinitely." For the first time, Earth is in danger of losing that ability. At the present rate that we are using its resources, our planet cannot maintain itself. The world's seas are a vital part of these resources, and it is important that we use them sustainably.

The seas face an increasing number of threats, including pollution, poor fishing practices, climate change, and poorly planned developments along coasts. The marine environment is always changing. Most of the changes are the result of human decisions and actions. Many of the images we see on television, on the Internet, and in newspapers and films show a gloomy future for our seas.

Huge oceans surround the continents of the world. Oceans and seas cover more than 70 percent of Earth's surface.

Map of the world's oceans

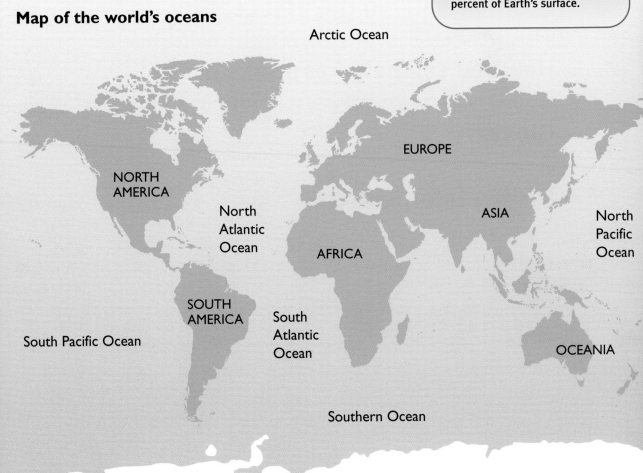

Arctic Ocean

EUROPE

NORTH AMERICA

North Atlantic Ocean

ASIA

North Pacific Ocean

AFRICA

SOUTH AMERICA

South Atlantic Ocean

South Pacific Ocean

OCEANIA

Southern Ocean

ANTARCTICA

Fish such as these cod are a vital source of food and income, but overfishing and pollution of the seas is threatening their existence.

We have the power to use the seas so that their resources are not damaged or reduced and so that whatever is used or removed can be renewed. This is called sustainable use and will keep our seas healthy, with productive fisheries and thriving marine life. Sustainable use of the seas will mean that while we are meeting our needs for the present, we will not stop people from being able to meet their needs from the seas in the future.

There are a wide range of possible solutions to the threats and problems facing the marine environment. How can these ensure that the future of our seas is sustainable?

The ocean's resources

Nearly all of the continents in the world are surrounded by shallow waters that extend beyond the land, known as the continental shelf. This shelf is hundreds of feet deep, unlike the open ocean, which reaches depths of thousands of feet. Sediment from the land is washed into the waters of the shelf by rivers and waves, where it provides food and nutrients for microscopic plants and animals called plankton. Larger animals, including great schools of fish, such as sardines, pilchards, and herring, feed on the plankton. We catch these fish for food. The continental shelf regions also contain the highest number of plants and animals that live on the ocean floor. It is estimated that more than 80 percent of all the ocean's resources lie on the continental shelf.

Food

Seas are a major source of food for people throughout the world. Coastal areas are breeding grounds for fish, crabs, mussels, prawns, and other marine life that many people rely on for food. These vital sources of food are now at risk because of over-harvesting, and stocks of many wild fish are declining. In contrast, fish and other seafood produced by marine aquaculture (farming of fish and other sea life) is increasing.

Aquaculture is now the fastest-growing food production sector in the world, but many marine farms are polluting coastal environments with waste food, fish droppings, and chemicals. Aquaculture can also damage local economies. Local fishermen often lose their livelihoods when marine farms replace the natural habitats fishermen used to fish in.

Livelihoods

The seas provide a livelihood for many millions of people through fishing and leisure activities such as boating and tourism. However, these uses of the sea are often unsustainable.

Fishing is important for the economy of local communities as well as national economies worldwide. An estimated 45 percent of the world catch is now traded internationally. However, the amount of fish the world's fishing boats are capable of catching is two and a half times more than the amount of fish the oceans can sustainably produce.

A fisherman in Sumatra casting his net. In some of the world's poorest coastal regions, fish are especially important, providing the main source of protein for more than a billion people.

For many tropical developing countries, such as those in the Pacific and Caribbean Oceans, coastal tourism is a major source of employment and money. But uncontrolled development due to coastal tourism is damaging coastal seas around the world.

Living on the edge

Around 60 percent of the world's human population lives within 40 miles (64 km) of the sea. Almost half of the world's cities with more than one million people are situated on estuaries. Pressures on seas and coasts are growing as people living and working there turn to them for food, leisure, and disposal of sewage and other waste. These pressures are resulting in increasingly unsustainable demands being made on the natural resources of coastal areas and seas.

Sea facts

▶ Seas cover 71 percent of Earth's surface.

▶ Some of the world's seas are vast—the Pacific, for example, covers half the globe.

▶ Seas account for 95 percent of all the space on the planet that is available to life.

▶ The seas make up nine-tenths of Earth's total water resources.

▶ Seawater quality is an important sign of the health of the environment.

▶ Humans have explored less than 10 percent of the seas.

▶ More people have traveled into space than have ventured into the deep of the oceans.

▶ We have better maps of the surface of the moon than of the seafloor.

San Francisco, California, on the coast of the Pacific Ocean. In the United States, about 53 percent of the population lives near the coast, and since 1970, about 2,000 homes per day have been built in coastal areas.

Biodiversity

The seas contribute enormously to the diversity of life. Representatives from every major group of plants and animals are found in the seas. Species range from the blue whale to the tiniest plankton. The seas are one of the world's major natural communities, known as biomes. The other biomes are fresh waters, deserts, forests, grasslands, and tundra.

Many of the creatures that live under the surface of the world's seas are amazingly beautiful. Marine sea slugs, for example, have an extraordinary range of colors and patterns—unlike their relatives that live on land. Sea slugs, such as these *Gymnodoris aurita* found in the Komodo National Park in the Indian Ocean, taste horrible, and their bright colors warn other animals not to eat them.

Ecosystems

Biomes have many different ecosystems. An ecosystem consists of all of the plants and animals in an area, together with their environment. The plants and animals interact with one another and with their environment. Species compete for space and food, eat one another, and live together in a complex web of relationships. Each living thing in an ecosystem has its own role to play.

Case Study: Albatross and long-lining

The growth in long-lining—baited fishing lines in the sea—is a deadly threat to all species of albatross. The albatross are attracted to the bait left for fish and get caught on the hooks themselves. More than 100,000 albatross may be killed every year in the Southern Ocean by illegal long-line fisheries catching Patagonian toothfish. This is a highly valuable fish sold in restaurants as Chilean sea bass. Such a level of deaths is unsustainable. Yet solutions as simple as trailing colored plastic streamers to scare off the birds could remove the danger from hooks on fishing lines. Illegal fishing not only harms seabirds, but also reduces fish stocks by taking too many fish.

Today, 20 of the 24 albatross species in the world are thought to be in danger of extinction in the near future. If fishing nations do not agree to use fishing methods that do not harm albatross and other seabirds, whole species may die out.

The black-browed albatross lives a roaming life over the sea, flying thousands of miles before coming to land to breed. Recent surveys have revealed that the black-browed albatross is now endangered. In the Falkland Islands, which are home to the majority of the world's population of black-browed albatross, breeding pairs of the bird fell from 458,000 in 1995 to 382,000 in 2005.

Ecosystems provide many invaluable and irreplaceable services from which people benefit. For instance, marine ecosystems regulate our climate. They absorb heat and redistribute it around the world, and provide rainwater for the land through the evaporation of seawater. Phytoplankton in the seas play a valuable role by absorbing carbon dioxide (the main gas that is causing global warming). During a process called photosynthesis, the phytoplankton convert carbon dioxide into oxygen, producing half of the world's supply of this essential gas.

The web of life in an ecosystem is easily disturbed by human interference and will fail if it does not stay balanced. If we are to continue to benefit from the services provided by the ecosystems of the seas, then we must use their resources sustainably.

Sea ecosystems

The range of marine ecosystems is hugely varied. There are beautiful coral reefs, ocean depths, rich estuaries, salt marshes, mangroves, seagrass beds, spectacular rocky coasts, and sandy shores. Each supports different plants and animals, and each faces different challenges in maintaining sustainability.

The deep seas

The ecosystem of the deep seafloor is vast. Around 60 percent of Earth's solid surface lies beneath oceans that are deeper than 3,300 feet (1,000 m). At the bottom of these seas, the waters are cold and dark because no light reaches there. Manned and remote-operated vehicles have only recently been able to reach the deep seafloor. There, they found huge expanses of soft sediments, seamounts that rise at least 3,300 feet (1,000 m), plumes of warm water rushing out of cracks in the seabed, and deep, steep-sided submarine canyons. It is likely that many species from deep-sea ecosystems are yet to be discovered.

Threats

Up until now, human activity has affected the deep seas very little compared to the rest of the planet. As natural resources on land and in the more easily reached areas of the seas are used up, pressures on the deep seas are increasing. For example, as fish stocks decline in the upper ocean, more and more fishing is taking place in the deeps. Deep-sea fish are long-lived and slow-growing and produce only a small number of young over a long period. The orange roughy, for instance, is 25 to 30 years old before it can breed, and it lives more than 100 years. If too many adult orange roughy are caught, it will be many years before the fish can breed again. This means that an orange roughy fishery is unsustainable, because more fish are taken than can be naturally replaced.

From the surface, oil rigs such as this one in the Gulf of Mexico do not seem to make much of an impact on the environment. Below the surface, however, the damage to the deep seabed can be massive.

Mangroves in Queensland, Australia. Traditionally, mangrove forests were sustainably used by many coastal communities to supply building materials, firewood, charcoal, food, and medicine.

Dumping of human wastes such as carbon dioxide could be a major threat to the deep seas in the future. Drilling for oil and gas is causing a considerable amount of damage around drilling sites. The future mining of minerals, especially manganese, which is used in the production of steel, is likely to seriously harm thousands of square miles of the ocean floor. Due to these harmful effects, the use of the natural resources of the deep seas is thought to be unsustainable until we understand them better.

Mangroves

Mangroves are trees and shrubs that grow in the tropics on wetlands that are regularly covered by the tides. The plants are highly adapted to a salty environment. Mangroves provide valuable nursery areas and food for many species of fish, crustaceans, and shellfish. Many animals find shelter in mangrove roots or branches. The trees are nesting sites for coastal birds. Mangroves in Bhitarkanika National Park, for example, support the largest breeding colony of water birds in India—including the Asian openbill stork. Mangroves help protect the shoreline and coral reefs by absorbing the energy of waves and wind in stormy weather. Mangrove plants and sediments have also been shown to absorb pollution, including heavy metals.

Threats and solutions

Mangrove forests once covered three-quarters of the coastlines of tropical and subtropical countries. Today, less than 50 percent of original mangrove forests remain, and half of those that remain are not in good condition. Global mangrove deforestation rates are now higher than those of tropical rain forests. Mangroves have often been cleared for tourist developments, and recently, shrimp aquaculture has also been a major cause of deforestation.

At the present time, less than one percent of mangroves are properly protected. By practicing sustainable shrimp aquaculture and raising awareness of the importance of mangroves, we could increase this figure and save the mangroves from disappearing altogether.

What are coral reefs?

Coral polyps are tiny animals with a hard skeleton made of calcium carbonate. Small algae grow inside the skeleton. Coral reefs are formed when large numbers of these skeletons join together. Coral reefs are one of the most spectacular and productive of ecosystems. The variety of life they support rivals that of the Amazon rain forest. Although coral reefs occupy less than .25 percent of the marine environment, they are home to 25 percent of all marine life.

Coral reef services

Coral reefs are estimated to provide around $28 billion per year in services that benefit people. In many coastal areas, they are natural breakwaters, protecting beaches and property on shorelines from wave action, storms, and floods. Reefs can generate high incomes from tourism. Tourists visiting the Great Barrier Reef in Australia, for example, spend almost a billion dollars a year.

Coral reefs are valuable nursery grounds for fish and help to maintain healthy fish stocks that provide food for thousands of coastal communities. Scientists have also found chemicals in reef creatures that can be used to treat cancer and HIV. There are many compounds that could still prove valuable to medicine.

Threats

Coral reefs are one of the world's fastest-declining ecosystems. More than 25 percent of all reefs have already been destroyed, and 50 to 70 percent of remaining reefs are threatened by human activities.

Often, so many fish are taken from a reef that its population cannot be sustained. This unbalances life in the coral reef ecosystem. Many current fishing practices are destructive and unsustainable. For instance, cyanide is frequently used to stun and capture large fish used in tropical aquariums and as food for restaurants. The chemical cloud produced in this process poisons smaller fish and coral polyps. Coral reefs are often dynamited to kill and harvest small fish. This fishing method seriously damages the reef.

Reefs are vital nurseries for about a quarter of the ocean's fish species and provide income and employment for local fishing communities and other fishermen.

Climate change is leading to an increase in sea temperatures. This increase in temperature kills the algae in coral polyps and eventually kills the polyps themselves, because they need the algae for food. The loss of algae causes the coral to lose its color and become white. This is known as bleaching. In 1998, bleaching occurred on reefs around the world, and in some regions, the resulting coral deaths reached 70 percent of reefs. Many scientists believe that global warming will bring more extreme weather. Heavy rainfall, which causes soil erosion and severe tropical storms, damages reefs. Coral reefs in tropical countries need to be in warm, shallow waters. Rising sea levels that result from climate change mean that some reefs could be in waters that are too deep.

Over the last 100 years, levels of carbon dioxide in the atmosphere have risen sharply due to the burning of fossil fuels. Some of the carbon dioxide dissolves in the oceans, forming carbonic acid. This makes the water more acidic, and the increased acidity is gradually dissolving the calcium carbonate skeletons of coral polyps. As a result of this, scientists have predicted that the Great Barrier Reef will disappear, or be dramatically changed forever, by 2050 or 2100.

Reefs are also suffering from coastal development, sewage, and chemical pollution, as well as from careless tourists who touch and damage them.

A sustainable future for coral

In order to try to ensure a sustainable future for coral reefs, we need to:

- create more protected areas
- reduce global warming so that coral reefs can have the stable climate they need
- encourage local fishing communities to use sustainable fishing methods
- gain the support of governments and communities worldwide to save coral reefs.

As tourists, we can help by supporting reef-friendly businesses, not eating reef fish, and being careful not to damage reefs when diving.

What are estuaries?

An estuary is a place where a river meets the sea. It is a body of water partly surrounded by land, where fresh water mixes with salt water. Although influenced by the tides, estuaries are protected from the full force of ocean waves, winds, and storms by reefs, islands, or thin strips of land, mud, or sand. Many different habitat types are found in and around estuaries, including shallow open waters, freshwater and saltwater marshes, sandy beaches, mud and sand flats, rocky shores, oyster reefs, mangrove forests, river deltas, tidal pools, seagrass and kelp beds, and wooded swamps.

The tidal, sheltered waters of estuaries support unique communities of plants and animals specially adapted for life at the edge of the sea. Estuarine environments are among the most productive on Earth. This means they produce biomass (living material) at a faster rate than many other ecosystems, including forests and grasslands. More than two-thirds of the fish and shellfish we eat spend some part of their lives in estuaries.

Salt marshes in estuaries can act as filters, keeping pollutants from the land from reaching the sea. They also protect land from flooding. Estuaries are popular tourist destinations, and millions of people visit them each year to boat, swim, bird-watch, and fish.

Threats

Estuaries are attractive to developers. In areas of high population, estuaries are dredged to provide harbors, marinas, and recreation resources. Alternatively, salt marshes are sometimes drained to make space to build homes, or for industry and farmland. On a global scale, more than half of all estuaries and other wetlands have been destroyed. Rising sea levels resulting from global warming threaten to submerge remaining undeveloped estuaries.

Saving estuaries

Sustainable management of estuaries will mean controlling the spread of new developments with the help of local communities. Pollution of rivers and streams that run into the estuaries will need to be stopped. Measures to reduce the impact of climate change (rising sea levels) will also help protect estuaries.

Estuaries such as this one in England may like empty wastelands, but they support a huge amount of marine life. Seals, shorebirds, fish, crabs, lobsters, shellfish, marine worms, and reptiles are just some of the animals that make their homes in and around estuaries.

Case Study: Salt marshes

Coastal marshes that are covered by most high tides are known as salt marshes. Only a few plants (mainly grasses) are adapted to live in such salty places that are so frequently flooded.

A food web is all of the food chains that are connected in an ecosystem. This food web diagram (below) shows the variety of plants and animals found in salt marshes along the coast of Georgia. All healthy ecosystems must have a balance between producers (living things that make food), consumers (living things that feed on others), and decomposers (living things that feed by breaking down dead plants and animals).

The main producers in salt marshes are microscopic plants called phytoplankton, which drift in the tidal currents, and algae, which are simple one-celled plants that live on rocks or logs in salt marshes. Cord grass, a salt-resistant plant, is another important producer in salt marshes.

Many consumers eat these producers. There are invertebrates, such as snails and crabs, a variety of fish species, and birds such as clapper rails. There are also some mammal visitors, such as raccoons.

Bacteria play a vital role in the ecosystem and are known as decomposers. They break down dead plants and animals in the salt marsh to form detritus, which is eaten by shrimps, mussels, and some crabs.

In this food web diagram, each plant or animal in the salt marsh ecosystem is linked to another by an arrow that points to the plant or animal that it eats to form a series of food chains. Most of the animals eat more than one type of plant or animal, so they feed in more than one food chain. In this way, many connections are made between the salt marsh food chains and form the salt marsh food web.

Salt marsh food web

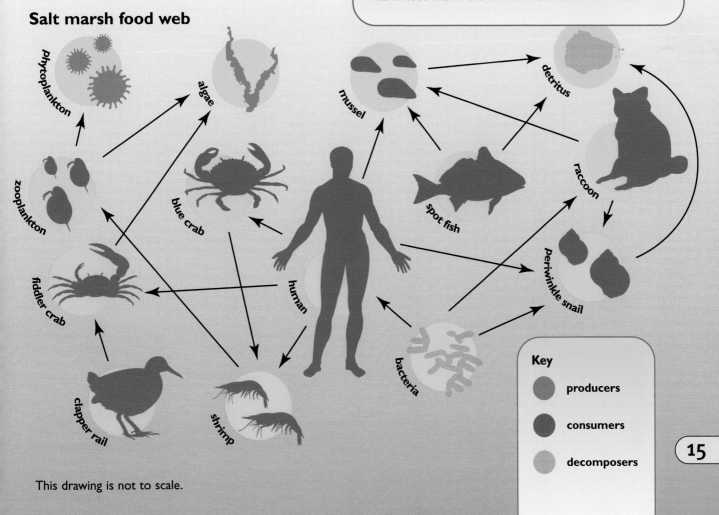

phytoplankton · algae · mussel · detritus · raccoon · zooplankton · blue crab · human · spot fish · periwinkle snail · fiddler crab · bacteria · clapper rail · shrimp

Key
- producers
- consumers
- decomposers

This drawing is not to scale.

Antarctic marine ecosystem

The Antarctic marine ecosystem lies in the Southern Ocean that encircles the South Pole and surrounds the continent of Antarctica. The seawater is rich in nutrients that rise to the surface and form food for plankton, which are eaten by small, shrimp-like creatures called krill. Krill are a vital part of the Antarctic food web and provide food for several species, including the blue whale and many fish. This has resulted in a particularly rich marine ecosystem.

The Convention on the Conservation of Antarctic Marine Living Resources (CCAMLR) manages the Antarctic marine living environment. It began in 1982 as part of the Antarctic Treaty System, which declared the continent a natural reserve devoted to peace and science.

CCAMLR aims to conserve the whole marine ecosystem. A species must be caught sustainably so that its population is not reduced—for example, by not taking very young fish, leaving a proportion to grow and breed in the future. Some species are dependent on other species for food, so this must also be taken into account when catching them.

Threats and solutions

Despite CCAMLR, the Southern Ocean is not being used sustainably. Overfishing is threatening the slow-growing, long-lived, high-value Patagonian toothfish. Up to 80 percent of the toothfish catch is thought to be from illegal sources. Krill are in danger, mainly from the fast-expanding fish farming industry that catches krill for feed. The loss of ozone in the upper atmosphere has led to an increase in ultraviolet light reaching the water. This has reduced the production of phytoplankton, on which krill depend. Krill feed under sea ice ledges, and global warming has shrunk sea ice by a quarter since the 1950s.

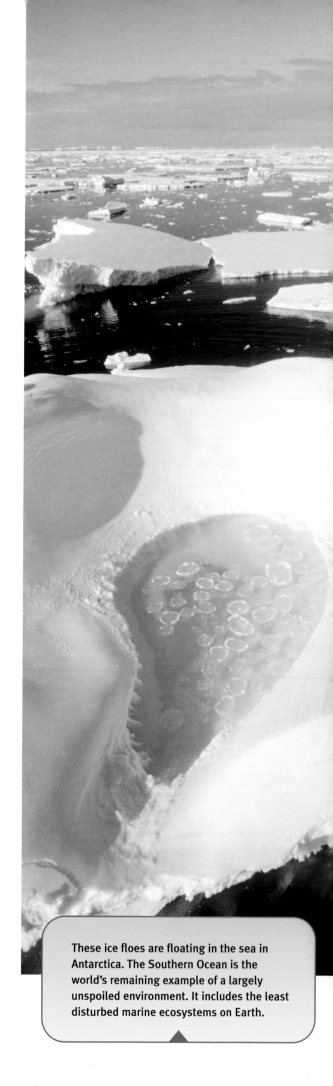

These ice floes are floating in the sea in Antarctica. The Southern Ocean is the world's remaining example of a largely unspoiled environment. It includes the least disturbed marine ecosystems on Earth.

There are fears that Antarctic minke whale numbers may have greatly declined in the Southern Ocean in the last 25 years, perhaps because of melting sea ice and reduced krill numbers. Despite the fact that the Southern Ocean is a whale sanctuary, Japan still catches 440 minke whales a year.

Tourist numbers have tripled in the past 10 years and are rapidly adding more pressure on the vulnerable Antarctic environment. The tourist industry has voluntary guidelines for protecting the environment. These could be improved upon by additional controls under the Antarctic Treaty. CCLAMR aims to set up large-scale marine protected areas throughout Antarctica so that different ecosystem types can be looked after properly.

Tourists visiting a chinstrap penguin colony on Halfmoon Island, Antarctica. Most tourists go to the two percent of the Antarctic that is ice-free. Visiting is concentrated when penguins and seals are breeding and are especially sensitive to disturbance.

Case Study: Bioprospecting in Antarctica

Bioprospecting is the search for genetic material from species that have successfully adapted to extreme environments. It is the latest commercial interest in Antarctica. For instance, Antarctic fish create their own antifreeze so that they do not freeze solid. This chemical can be extracted and used to make ice cream or for the transport and storage of blood. Bioprospecting discoveries such as these can make huge amounts of money. The problem is that no one country owns these resources, so who should get the benefit from them? International cooperation under the Antarctic Treaty could establish a way of controlling bioprospecting before it grows any bigger.

Threats to seas

The world's seas are in real danger. There is an urgent need for fisheries to become sustainable and for pollution and human damage to be reduced. Overfishing, loss of breeding habitats, modern fishing methods, poor management of fisheries, pollution, and climate change are all contributing to the disappearance of fish from the oceans. Many fishing communities around the world are threatened as fish stocks decline.

Overfishing

Three-quarters of the world's fish stocks are overexploited. For hundreds of years, fishermen have traveled to distant seas, but in the last 60 years, the size and catching power of boats has increased dramatically. As fish stocks are overfished in home waters, more and more fishermen are searching around the world for different kinds of fish to catch and for more productive seas. Soon, these waters will be overexploited, too.

Since 1950, the world catch of fish has steadily increased by several million tons.

Source: United Nations Food and Agriculture Statistics o

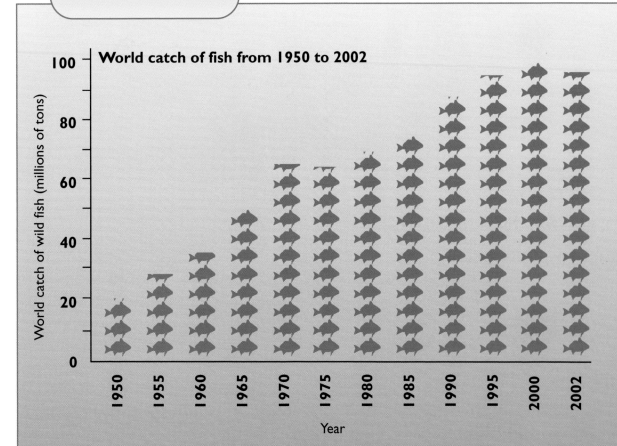

World catch of fish from 1950 to 2002

Today's technology enables fishing fleets to track down the rarest of fish and catch them. Overfishing by foreign fleets is robbing many local people who rely on fish for their livelihoods and as an important source of food. Of the hundreds of thousands of ships around the world, approximately 1,300 are likely to be fishing illegally, going against international or local agreements, or fishing in protected areas. As fish populations are severely reduced, many fish do not live long enough to become mature. Only a small percentage of wild cod reach breeding age. Of the one-year-old cod in the North Atlantic, for example, only four percent will reach the breeding age of four to five years.

By-catch

Inefficient fishing methods waste at least a quarter of the fish that are caught. These are fish that are caught accidentally and are known as "by-catch." As much as 33 million tons (30 million t) a year of by-catch are being thrown over the side of fishing boats. These fish are dead or dying.

Industrial fishing

"Industrial fish" are small fish used to feed livestock, chickens, and farmed fish. The impact of industrial fishing is of great concern throughout the world because these small fish are the food of a wide range of marine predators in the wild. These predators include larger fish, seabirds, seals, dolphins, and whales. Too many "industrial fish" are being caught, putting catches of other commercial fish and wildlife populations at risk.

Impacts of fishing methods

The seabed is made up of different kinds of important habitats for plants and animals. These habitats include muddy bottoms, reefs, and rocky outcrops. Fishing gear such as trawls and dredges that are towed across the seabed can destroy these habitats and their wildlife. At least once a year, 90 percent of the North Sea is trawled. The result of this repeated trawling is that little life is left on the seabed.

Worldwide, nearly 1,000 whales, dolphins, and porpoises are estimated to die every day after they become entangled in fishing gear. When trapped by fishing lines or nets, they are unable to swim, so they cannot reach the surface to breathe. Fishing gear floating in the sea is now believed to be the main threat to the survival of these marine mammals.

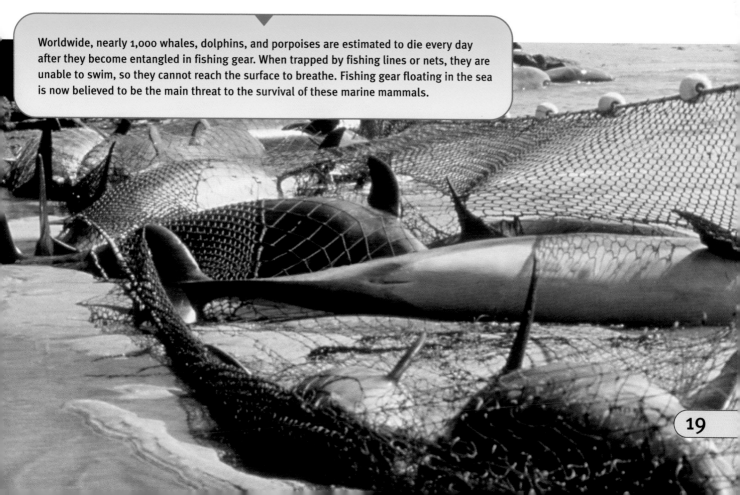

Aquaculture

If aquaculture is to be sustainable, it needs to be managed much better. Although many people believe that fish farming relieves the pressure on ocean fisheries, the reverse is actually true. At present, aquaculture uses 70 percent of the world's production of fish oil and 34 percent of fish meal. This means that enormous amounts of wild fish are caught to produce the fish oil and fish meal that are needed to feed the fish produced by aquaculture. This obviously contributes to the threat of overfishing.

Aquaculture also presents other threats to sustainability, such as pollution. At the present time, many farmed fish are diseased or infested with parasites. If the fish escape into the wild, they can pass these diseases on to wild fish. The chemicals used on fish farms to treat diseases and parasites can pollute coastal waters. Waste food and fish droppings from fish farms may silt the seabed and use up vital oxygen in seawater as they decay. Nutrients from the waste and fish feed can enrich waters, leading to large growths of algae, called algal blooms, that may be poisonous to other marine life.

Fish farms need the shelter of bays to avoid damage from storms and currents. Here, they may be in direct competition with marine protected areas for space or may spoil landscapes that were undeveloped before.

Annual sales of shrimps and prawns now amount to $46 billion to $57 billion worldwide and are growing at 9 percent a year. Shrimps and prawns are produced by intensive fish farming in some developing countries in Asia and Latin America, mainly for the U.S., Europe, and Japan. This trade has led to serious environmental damage as well as pollution.

Poorly planned industrial-scale aquaculture, such as these shrimp farms in Thailand, can lead to the severe destruction of marine habitats. The shrimp farms have replaced huge areas of mangroves. This has led to social hardship, as many local people used to live and work among mangroves, and the shrimp farms cannot provide enough jobs to make up for this.

Climate change

Earth retains its temperature thanks to
a blanket of gases, known as greenhouse
gases, which trap heat near Earth's surface
that would otherwise escape into space. The
"greenhouse effect" occurs naturally and
makes life on Earth possible.

Human activities are increasing the
concentration of naturally occurring
greenhouse gases in the atmosphere,
especially carbon dioxide. About two-thirds
of greenhouse gas emissions come from the
carbon dioxide given off when we burn fossil
fuels such as coal, gas, and oil. Most scientists
believe the increased amounts of greenhouse
gases are causing the world to heat up
unnaturally and the weather to become more
extreme. The heating process is often referred
to as global warming, and the overall effect is
known as climate change.

Global warming has led to a rise in sea
temperatures that has caused seawater to
expand and sea levels to rise. Glaciers
worldwide are melting and contributing to
this rise. Scientists predict that sea levels will
increase by as much as .2 inches (5 mm) per
year over the next 100 years as a result of
global warming. This is clearly a threat to
coastal areas around the world.

Rising sea levels threaten entire nations
on low-lying islands in the Pacific and
Indian Oceans, such as this one in the
Maldives. Salty seawater is already making
groundwater undrinkable on some islands.

Climate change is believed to be causing
major changes in the level and distribution
of plankton. Since plankton form the basis
of fish food chains, these changes could also
affect fish stocks such as cod. About a third
of the carbon dioxide in the atmosphere is
thought to dissolve in the oceans. This
produces carbonic acid, which damages the
growth of coral reefs and plankton containing
calcium carbonate.

Warming of seawater is affecting the
migration of some species, such as the
Atlantic salmon, and the breeding of others,
such as the harp seal. Polar bears are now
having problems finding enough food on
Arctic sea ice during the winter because the
ice is melting earlier and forming later, giving
the bears less time to hunt.

Climate change may even result in the
change in direction of ocean currents. This
could have drastic consequences, as the
currents control our weather, preventing
it from becoming too hot or too cold.

Case Study: *Prestige* oil spill, Spain

On November 23, 2002, the *Prestige* oil tanker sank in 9,800 feet (3,000 m) of water off the Spanish coast. The tanker came to rest on an underwater mountain that is very rich in sea life, including many species not yet identified. A total of 70,000 tons (64,000 t) of oil leaked into the sea. Damage to fishing, tourism, and the environment along 1,865 miles (3,000 km) of coastline polluted by the spill may last for more than 10 years and cost around $4 billion.

These workers are cleaning up after the *Prestige* oil tanker disaster. The livelihoods of around 30,000 fishermen were directly hit by the spill. After the fisheries reopened, some local fishermen reported an 80 percent reduction in catches.

A large amount of oil settled on the seabed of shallower waters. From there, it entered marine food chains through living things that feed on sediments. The pollutants eventually ended up in animals, such as octopuses and crabs that are caught for food. Some 300,000 seabirds (mainly common guillemots and Atlantic puffins) are estimated to have died from the oil spill. This was one of the deadliest man-made disasters to wildlife ever to have occurred in Europe.

Accidents at sea are hard to prevent, but strengthening safety laws could be one measure to protect these sensitive and vulnerable areas of the sea.

Oil pollution

Oil spills at sea can have serious immediate consequences for wildlife and the environment. Many seabirds are killed, and their populations may be slow to recover. Chemicals from oil are also linked to the recent high increase in fish diseases.

In fact, tanker accidents actually account for less than five percent of the oil pollution that gets into the sea. More oil pollution runs into the sea via streams and rivers each year from leaking cars than was released by the *Exxon Valdez* tanker accident in 1989.

This accident in Alaska spilled 42,000 tons (38,000 t) of oil. Ships release about half of the oil entering the world's seas, much of which is deliberately flushed into the sea as tankers clean their tanks. Most of the rest comes from land sources, or from oil and gas exploration and drilling at sea. Oil covering beaches is costly to remove and can lead to a loss in tourist trade that is damaging to the local economy.

Sea dumping and sea wastes

About 80 to 90 percent of the material dumped at sea comes from dredging and currently amounts to hundreds of millions of tons a year. Most of the material is dredged from harbors and rivers to keep them from silting up. The dredged material is usually dumped in coastal areas, often smothering the seabed and plant and animal life growing there. About 10 percent of the dredged material is polluted with heavy metals, oil, pesticides, and other chemicals that can poison marine life and our food sources.

The common guillemot was the seabird species most affected by the *Prestige* oil spill. Birds can be killed by swallowing even small amounts of oil, or because their feathers have become oil-covered, preventing them from moving around or flying.

Source: International Tanker Owners Pollution Federation Ltd.

Oil spills greater than 700 tons, 1970 to 2004

The average number of large spills per year has decreased sharply since the 1970s due to better safety regulations. However, large spills are still causing great environmental damage, especially in areas of the sea that are particularly vulnerable.

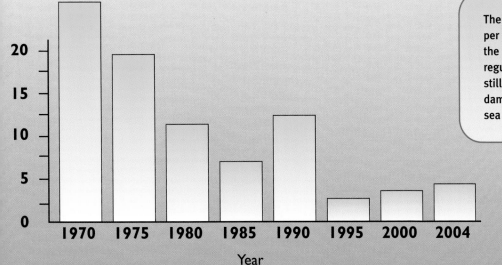

Year

23

Sea pollution from land

People have treated seas as a dumping ground for thousands of years, with little care for the damage this may cause. Most of the wastes produced by human activities eventually reach the sea.

Sewage is one of the most widespread and serious pollutants. Untreated sewage is a health hazard, yet many parts of the world have no sewage systems.

Nutrients, such as nitrogen, from sewage, fertilizers used in farming, fumes from vehicles, and wastes from factories can over-enrich coastal waters. The nutrients lead to a rapid growth of algal blooms. When these blooms die, the decomposing plants reduce oxygen in the water, sometimes to dangerously low levels, killing fish and other marine life. A recent United Nations report identified nearly 150 oxygen-starved or "dead zones" in the world's seas.

Nearly a third of dead zones lie off the U.S., but there are also clusters around Europe, Japan, China, Brazil, Australia, and New Zealand. The size and number of these dead zones are rising, and they are fast becoming major threats to fisheries.

A wide range of chemical wastes from industry, farming, and homes eventually enters the sea. These wastes include pesticides, heavy metals, plastic, and other dangerous man-made materials. Some chemicals remain in the environment for a very long time and do not easily break down. Toxic chemicals in seawater are absorbed by plankton, which are eaten by tiny invertebrates. These invertebrates are in turn eaten by fish, which are food to seals and seabirds. In this way, the chemicals build up in food chains and threaten species.

In the Arctic, toxic chemicals are being passed through the food chain from seals to polar bears. The polar bears' resistance to infections is reduced, and female bears can pass on the toxins, in their milk, to cubs. This reduces the cubs' chances of survival.

Plastic pollution

Every year, about 1 million seabirds and 100,000 marine mammals (including 30,000 seals) are killed by plastic marine litter worldwide. At least 177 marine species, mainly seabirds, are known to have eaten plastics and other litter.

As many as 45,000 pieces of plastic litter are estimated to be floating on every square mile (2.5 sq km) of the world's seas.

Plastic dumped on land can be carried along streams or blown hundreds of miles into the sea.

A plastic bottle can take 450 years to break down.

Marine turtles like this one are particularly badly affected by plastic pollution. Many turtles have been found dead with plastic bags in their stomachs. One dead turtle found off Hawaii had more than 1,000 pieces of plastic in its stomach, including part of a comb, a toy truck wheel, and nylon rope.

Chemical pollution is now a global threat. Even the world's most remote regions are affected. Surprisingly, animals in the Arctic are seriously threatened by very high levels of pollution. Air and water carry pollutants from the south. Once they reach the Arctic, pollutants are trapped by polar ice and are gradually released into the environment during melting periods, even years later.

The majority of pollutants come from sources on land. This means that coastal waters, the most important for marine life, are the most polluted. This has serious consequences for fisheries and fishermen. Most of the global catch of marine fish is taken within 200 miles (320 km) of a coastline. Coastal wetlands, including estuaries, mangroves, and coral reefs, are nursery areas for fish and other sea life.

Levels of waste in the world's seas are increasing almost everywhere. To ensure long-term sustainable use of the seas, pollutants must be stopped or reduced. The development of new technologies to reduce or process waste will help. The ideal solution, however, would be to consume less, and so produce less waste. There are controls on waste in many countries, although illegal dumping of waste is a problem.

Fish from sustainable sources

Unsustainable fishing is drastically reducing fish populations around the world. Wiser management of fishing grounds could ensure that the oceans continue to produce valuable food supplies worldwide and that coastal communities are healthy.

Marine protected areas

Marine protected areas provide food, shelter, and breeding grounds for fish and other sea life. Many marine protected areas are highly successful in increasing commercial fish catches. For example, in the Edmunds Underwater Park, in Washington, lingcod fish produced 20 times more eggs than in surrounding areas that were fished.

A group of seven islands of coral and sand form the Dry Tortugas Marine Reserve. The area is famous for its bird and marine life.

Case Study: Dry Tortugas Marine Reserve, Florida Keys

The Tortugas are a spectacular ecosystem of islands, beaches, and coral reefs. They are home to an incredible number of species, such as the rare green turtle, black coral, and goliath grouper fish. The Tortugas are also an important fish nursery for fishing grounds hundreds of miles away, as well as in the Florida Keys.

By the late 1990s, commercial fishing was seriously threatening some key species in the Tortugas, such as the black grouper fish. Visitors to the Tortugas who were fishing for pleasure added to the pressure on fish numbers.

In 1997, conservationists, scientists, fishermen, and divers decided to work together to set up the Tortugas as a marine reserve. In 2001, after many meetings and much discussion among the different groups of interested people, 200 square miles (518 sq km) were declared protected. No fish or other wildlife can now be taken from this area.

The brown pelican can be found year-round in the coastal waters of the Florida Keys Marine Reserve. Like all pelicans, it has a long beak with a huge pouch attached to it. Its pouch can hold three times as much as its stomach can. The brown pelican uses the pouch to catch fish and also to cool itself, since the pouch is full of blood vessels, which can lose heat near the surface of the skin.

Marine protected areas are being recognized more and more as vital for conservation. Even so, only .5 percent of the world's marine environment is protected, compared to almost 13 percent of land. The way that marine protected areas are managed varies from place to place. In some cases, the agreements on management (for example, how many fish can be caught) are informal and not enforced by law. Around 75 percent of the world's marine protected areas suffer from little or no proper management, and fishing is permitted in almost all protected areas. The Worldwide Fund for Nature (WWF) is among the organizations campaigning for at least 10 percent of marine areas to be under some form of official protection by 2012.

A commercial fisherman in the Tortugas:

"When we first heard about marine reserves, there was a lot of fear. We didn't believe that they had much to offer us commercial fishermen. We felt that marine reserves were being forced upon us. However, once people got involved in the process, the fear started to fade away. Everyone was involved in planning the reserve from the start. All of us had a chance to raise our concerns and thoughts about the reserve.

Developing a plan that everyone could live with was not easy. With divers, recreational fishermen, commercial fishermen, and conservationists in the room, there were a lot of different interests to deal with. But as the process went on, it became clear to everyone that a reserve could provide some real benefits, both for fisheries and conservationists. People got to know each other and recognize each other's needs and concerns. As a result, it became a little easier to compromise.

In the end, everyone agreed on one proposal. I'm sure no one came out with exactly what they had hoped for, but the important thing was that we had a reserve proposal that everyone can live with. Now it's up to us to help make it work."

No-take zones

A "no-take zone" is an area closed to fishing. If fish are left undisturbed, they can usually breed and increase their populations quickly. No-take zones are already successful in the U.S. and New Zealand. In Ucunivanua village in Fiji, the local people set up a no-take zone for one of their fishing species—the clam. After 5 years of protection, clams were 18 times more common in the no-take zone, and 7 times more common in the fished zone, than before the no-take zone was set up. Fishermen started finding bigger clams than anyone had seen for many years. The project has been so popular that other communities in Fiji have set up no-take zones in their fishing grounds, too.

"We are not looking for a quick fix. Protecting fish breeding grounds is vital to the long-term survival of the fishing fleet. The measures we want are really long-term. But we are prepared to take serious action to reduce fish deaths."

Fisheries Minister

"If the fishing grounds are closed, even temporarily, we won't last another year. And what then? Me or my 12 crew have never done anything except fish."

Fisherman

Sustainable fishing methods are vital to maintain rural coastal communities like this one in the village of Fishoek, South Africa.

Control of fishing efforts

If the number of fishing boats or the time spent fishing is reduced, then fewer fish will be caught. This is an effective way to help fish populations recover and is being used in the European Union. In Scotland, the center of the UK fishing industry, $43 million was offered to 108 fishing boat owners to remove their boats from service and give up their fishing licences in December 2001. This is called "decommissioning." Most Scottish fishermen accept the need for European governments to limit the amount of fish caught for the future but feel that decommissioning is killing the current industry.

Catch control

Each year, scientists in the European Union recommend the catch limit allowed for each fish species. However, this controls only the number of fish that are kept by the fishermen, not all of the fish that they have caught, so it is not the most efficient way to manage fishing. Many of the caught fish are thrown back into the sea dead because they are too small or the wrong kind of fish.

The challenge for governments and other organizations is to balance the immediate needs of fishermen with the long-term needs of the environment.

> *"This vessel is my life's work; now it's going to be cut up. The boat's 9 years old, but there's still 20 or 30 years' life left in her, and yet she's going to be ripped to pieces and melted down. This is just a waste of money—it doesn't make sense."*
>
> Quote from a fisherman when his boat was taken out of service

> *"Stocks of fish are at risk of falling to levels at which production of young will be reduced forever. There is a danger of ever fewer fish producing even fewer young. By closing fishing grounds for one or two seasons, fish populations will have a fighting chance to recover."*
>
> Scientist

Howth fishing port in Dublin Bay, Ireland. Boats may be kept in harbor for fixed periods, resulting in fishermen losing valuable income. Boats may even be scrapped altogether, and then fishermen lose their jobs as well as their boats.

29

Sustainable aquaculture

By 2020, aquaculture could account for almost half of all fish harvested. Even today, for some species, such as salmon, farmed production is now greater than the wild harvest.

In recent years in the U.S., where the demand for sea fish has never been greater, there is a great opportunity to expand marine aquaculture. The government aims to increase the value of the industry from $900 million a year to $5 billion by 2025. The number of jobs in aquaculture should increase from 180,000 to 600,000. At the same time, the development of ways to safeguard the environment is planned. A code of conduct for responsible aquaculture has been drawn up.

In order to be sustainable, aquaculture must be combined with natural ecosystems and provide benefits for local people.

Only native species that need little or no fish meal or oils should be farmed, in order to avoid putting pressure on natural resources. Damaging effects on the surrounding ecosystem can be reduced by growing several species together—the wastes from one species becoming food for another.

In the Bay of Fundy in Canada, for example, salmon, kelp seaweed, and blue mussels are being successfully farmed together. The nitrogen-rich wastes from salmon provide valuable nutrients for kelp and blue mussels. Farming all three together has reduced problems from salmon wastes and increased the growth rates of kelp and blue mussels.

The waste from Atlantic salmon provides valuable nutrients for the kelp and mussels in the Bay of Fundy in Canada. Not only have their growth rates increased, but because they are using up the waste, seawater pollution is also reduced.

Farming of Atlantic salmon in Scotland has increased fivefold since the 1990s. New guidelines went into effect in Scotland in 2005 that will allow increases only to companies that can guarantee high-quality production with the least impact on the environment.

The quality of marine water should be protected by using chemicals as little as possible and by cleaning up waste food and fish wastes. Fish farms some distance out to sea are being successfully developed in Puerto Rico. Strong ocean currents carry waste away from these fish farms. The greater depth of water offshore is able to dilute pollutants from fish farms better than shallower inshore waters. In this way, offshore farms are currently less harmful than those inshore.

Farms should be located in places where they do not damage the landscape, and their size should be limited. Sustainable aquaculture should benefit local communities by producing food that they can afford. Traditional jobs and local people's views—and their access to the sea—should be respected when building new marine farms.

Inland marine farms

One new farming method is to grow marine plants and animals in salt water that is continually circulated. This provides a more sustainable form of aquaculture because the fish wastes and chemicals are not released into the environment. These farms are based on land, not in the sea. Although not combined with a natural ecosystem, this is an alternative method that can be sustainable.

A five-year research program into land-based marine farms is currently underway in Florida. If successful, there will be opportunities for marine farms on inland sites throughout the southern U.S.

Marine Stewardship Council

The Marine Stewardship Council (MSC) is a groundbreaking project created in response to the world fisheries crisis. It was set up through a partnership between WWF and Unilever, one of the world's largest commercial buyers of fish. The MSC aims to ensure the long-term future of fish stocks and the health of the marine environment on which they depend. It is an independent, nonprofit organization working to promote responsible fisheries worldwide.

Working with experts from around the world, the MSC developed a set of global standards to evaluate whether fisheries are being managed sustainably. If fisheries meet the MSC's strict standards, they can carry the MSC logo. All fisheries, large and small, anywhere in the world can apply to the MSC to be certified as sustainable.

Fish, especially oily fish, are an essential part of a healthy diet, and the demand to provide fish for food is as great as ever. Previously, many fish buyers in shops and restaurants were aware of overfishing and would have liked to buy fish that were harvested sustainably, but they could not find the information they needed.

Chefs are helping sustainability, too. For example, through the Chefs Collaborative in the U.S., chefs are promoting the use of sustainable (responsibly caught) fish and local ingredients.

WWF is showing that MSC certification can conserve fisheries and improve the lives of fishermen. The MSC program also benefits fishermen who fish in a sustainable way by bringing in new customers and more opportunities for selling their catch.

At the traditional fish market at Karakoy in Istanbul, Turkey, fishermen sell fresh fish from their boats and along the docks.

More than 100 major seafood businesses, fishing groups, and conservation organizations now back the MSC. Alaskan pollock, New Zealand hoki, hake from South Africa and Chile, herring from the Thames estuary in England, and red rock lobster from Mexico are just a few of the MSC certified fisheries around the world.

> *"The MSC's program is based on respect and partnership with the fishing industry to accomplish change—a concept and practice our company wholeheartedly endorses."*
>
> Fish retailer

> *"We need an organization like the MSC to check and monitor the sustainability of our seafood so we may encourage the fishing industry and the consumer to support proper fish management."*
>
> Chef

> *"The MSC is our best hope for using the vast power of fish buyers to restore abundant and sustainable populations of sea fisheries and other wildlife."*
>
> Conservationist

A fishermen tends to a net on a factory trawler in the Bering Sea, Alaska, fishing for Alaskan pollock. The Alaskan pollock fishery is one of the largest in the world. It is the largest U.S. fishery, accounting for around a third (by weight) of all the fish caught in the country. In 2004, a panel of international marine scientists and fisheries experts agreed that the Alaskan pollock fishery was being sustainably and responsibly managed and could be given the Marine Stewardship Council label.

Sustainable tourism

Tourism means "travel undertaken for pleasure." It is one of the world's largest and fastest-growing industries. If developed sustainably, tourism can help conservation and environmental protection, as well as benefit local communities. It can raise awareness of the environment and can help pay for protection of natural areas. Unfortunately, much tourist development is both uncontrolled and badly planned.

Around the world, coastal tourist developments such as hotels, restaurants, shops, marinas, and roads have often led to increased pollution, soil erosion, and waste discharges into the sea, resulting in loss of natural habitats and wildlife. Even watching sea life can be harmful. In New Zealand, more than a third of a million visitors a year take part in marine tourism, and watching the New Zealand fur seal is a major attraction. However, recent research has found that tourists often disturb fur seals, and the current guidelines that advise visitors on behavior need major changes.

Without realizing it, we can sometimes be disturbing the natural way of life of some animals, such as the New Zealand fur seal, just by watching them. Greater understanding is needed for us to be truly responsible tourists.

Large marinas crammed with boats have grown at numerous harbors around the world, such as here in Monaco. The uncontrolled development of marinas results in pollution from wastewater from boats and loss of wildlife habitats.

In many cases, the bulk of tourists' money does not benefit the area they visit. When tourists travel on an all-inclusive package tour, about 80 percent of the money they have paid goes to airlines, hotels, and other international companies. Even if a tourist spends money directly in a vacation spot, it is often spent on goods that were imported to meet foreign tourists' demands. Although tourism can provide employment for local people, this is often just for the tourist season, which may last for only part of the year. Much employment in the tourism industry is low-skilled and therefore low-paid.

Local people can be affected in other ways, too. Fishing communities inhabited the coast of Penang, in Malaysia, 25 years ago. Today, the area has been taken over by tourists and beach hotels. Tourism sometimes results in the overconsumption of natural resources, such as water and wood. In the Seychelles, for example, high tourist demands for water cause severe shortages for local people.

What is sustainable tourism?

Sustainable tourism meets the needs of present tourists and places they are visiting now, while protecting and improving opportunities for the future. Sustainable tourism does not damage wildlife or the environment and is carried out so that each of these has the ability for renewal. Sustainable tourism respects the rights of people in the host country. Local communities need to have an equal share in the economic benefits of tourism. For example, hotels and other accommodations for visitors should be owned and run by local people. Local people should be directly involved in decisions about tourist developments where they live.

The fastest growth in tourism is now in ecotourism, which is responsible travel to natural areas that conserves the environment and improves the welfare of local people. The best way to identify truly sustainable tour operators is to look for those that have been certified. For example, Costa Rica, Brazil, and the Arctic all have certified sustainable tourism programs, and the Sustainable Tourism Certification Network of the Americas has 62 members in 19 countries.

Green turtle tourism on Bali

The green turtle is an endangered species that breeds on the beaches of Bali, an island in Indonesia. Most people on Bali are Hindus and have sacrificed green turtles for religious reasons for centuries. Hindus on Bali have also become used to eating turtles as part of their diet. As a result, nesting green turtles have seriously declined on the island. To meet the demand for turtles on Bali, as many as 25,000 are imported each year—despite a ban on the turtle trade under international and Indonesian laws.

Turtle ecotourism is now being used as a way of conserving green turtles in Bali. Since 1994, a turtle release program has been in place in Pemuteran in northwest Bali, which has become a popular destination for tourists to view marine turtles. The program has released more than 1,600 young turtles into the wild. Tourists pay a sum to release a green turtle into the wild and receive a certificate recognizing their contribution to marine turtle conservation.

This green turtle is nesting on the beach at Ascension Island. Marine turtles are an excellent species for wildlife tourism because they can be easily watched when they come ashore to nest.

The program provides an alternative income for local turtle egg hunters, who are offered twice the street price of turtle eggs on Bali. The local egg hunters find the marine turtle nests. The eggs are then transferred to an incubation site that is protected from predators, beach erosion, and poachers. In this way, the release program protects the turtle eggs and young turtles after they have hatched. At the same time, it provides an educational experience for tourists.

Adopt a nest program

WWF has started an "adopt a nest" program in Perancak village in Bali. Visiting tourists are "sold" nests on the beach where turtles are allowed to hatch naturally. Tourists receive a certificate of adoption with updated information on the nesting program. This program gives tourists an opportunity to contribute to marine turtle conservation. The money from the program is used to protect marine turtle nesting beaches and to provide alternative incomes for local communities.

Case Study: Ecotourism in Costa Rica

While many developing nations are focusing on industrialization, Costa Rica has turned to ecotourism for economic development. Although a small country less than half the size of England, Costa Rica has incredible biodiversity, scenic beaches, and exotic wildlife. Each year, the nation's tourist industry brings in about 1 million visitors and provides about $856 million, making it the country's second-largest source of income.

Ecotourism has encouraged the increase of Costa Rica's protected areas, which now cover 21 percent of the country. Watching turtles come ashore to lay their eggs is a popular ecotourism activity in Costa Rica. Six of the world's seven marine turtle species nest in the country. Guides go along with tourists to make sure the turtles are not disturbed. Some hotels near turtle nesting areas reduce lights close to the beach that could frighten female turtles and stop them from coming ashore.

Costa Rica is a popular tourist destination for foreign visitors because of beautiful beaches, such as this one at Playa Brazilito. It began a Certification of Sustainable Tourism program that helps visitors find the most environmentally friendly parks and resorts.

Orca watching around the San Juan Islands

Orcas belong to a family of marine mammals called cetaceans, which also includes dolphins, porpoises, and whales. Orcas, also known as killer whales, are some of the fastest mammals in the seas and can swim up to 30 miles (48 km) per hour. Their acrobatics and inquisitive behavior make them one of the most exciting of all cetaceans.

In recent years, watching orcas around the San Juan Islands, in the boundary waters of Washington and British Columbia, has become hugely popular. Each year, more than half a million people go on whale-watching boats here. If orca watching is to be sustainable, however, it is very important that the large numbers of people who watch these wonderful cetaceans do not disturb them and allow the orcas to live normal lives.

Whale and Dolphin Watching Code of Conduct:

▶ Don't spend longer than 15 minutes near cetaceans

▶ Keep speeds low and keep a steady direction

▶ Never drive head on to, move between, or separate cetaceans

▶ Keep your distance—don't get closer than 300 feet (90 m), or 600 feet (180 m) if another boat is present

▶ Use extra caution around mothers and young

▶ Never try to swim with wild cetaceans

Orcas often swim at very fast speeds toward the surface so that they can jump out of the water in a spectacular display before landing again with a huge splash.

If boats approach too closely, orcas can suffer from noise pollution. Like other cetaceans, orcas send out high-pitched sounds and listen to differences in the echoes that return in order to find their prey. Too much underwater noise from boats makes finding prey harder, so the orcas are forced to swim longer, using up more energy. Too many boats disturb orcas and can even result in collisions.

If carried out responsibly, orca watching can be a valuable and sustainable use of the marine environment, making a real contribution to orca conservation. Whale watching gives people the chance to learn about and appreciate marine life. As more people become aware of the importance of the marine environment, more of them will be inspired to help care for it.

Case Study: Marine tourism in Scotland

With more than 8,000 marine species in Scotland's waters, there is plenty of wildlife to be seen. Scotland has more than a third of the world's population of gray seals, 24 dolphin and whale species, basking sharks, and leatherback turtles. Marine tourism contributes greatly to the Scottish economy. One small sector—whale watching on Scotland's west coast—is worth as much as $20 million a year.

On the island of Mull, tourism is the largest employer, and whale watching is a key part of the economy, bringing in $1 million a year. Whale watching can be very important for some small rural communities that have few sources of income.

Whales and dolphins are Scotland's number-one wildlife attraction. An estimated quarter of a million tourists are involved with whale tourism activities each year in west Scotland.

Sustainability in the 21st century

At present, there are numerous separate laws and policies that try to protect the marine environment. Regulations are at global, regional, and national levels. Many of them try to ensure a sustainable future for the seas. The United Nations Convention on the Law of the Sea encourages sustainable ocean use and includes controls on sources of pollution from land, for example. Only a few countries have not agreed to this law, including the U.S. Although present regulations have helped to reduce overexploitation of our seas, in most cases, they are not effective enough to ensure sustainable use. The large number of laws controlling and managing the world's seas causes problems. Many laws are disconnected and often conflict to cater to different interests.

In 2002, the World Summit on Sustainable Development considered marine issues. Actions agreed on by the summit to improve sustainability of the seas included:

- encouraging the management of whole ecosystems in the seas
- an urgent international plan of action for the management of fisheries
- stopping subsidies (providing funds) that contribute to illegal fishing
- developing programs to stop the loss of marine biodiversity
- making the Global Program of Action for the Protection of the Marine Environment from Land-based Activities more effective
- regularly assessing the state of the global marine environment.

In 1996, Canada was the first country to pass an Oceans Act. Its goals are to use the resources of Canada's three oceans, the Atlantic, Pacific, and Arctic, while involving fishermen and industry, and maintaining sustainability.

People and reefs—a partnership

The International Coral Reef Action Network (ICRAN) is working to stop and reverse the decline in the health of the world's coral reefs. ICRAN promotes partnerships between communities, governments, and other stakeholders to protect and manage coral reefs. By working closely with local coastal communities, ICRAN provides support and resources to help them improve their management of reefs. A management plan was successfully developed with involved parties in the Malindi and Watamu Marine National Park and Reserve in Kenya, for example. Sustainably managed sites are being used to demonstrate success to others in each region. These demonstration sites share knowledge and management practices with other coral reef communities through local and regional workshops.

Since 2000, New Zealand has had an Oceans Policy that focuses on wisely managing the health of the oceans. In addition to actions taken by governments and other authorities, the direct involvement of local communities, which depend on the marine environment for their livelihoods, is essential if the future of the world's seas is to be sustainable.

These villagers in Segheraghi in the Solomon Islands are tending to a clam nursery as part of an ICRAN aquaculture project. The young clams are reared in the protective cages, increasing survival rates by reducing the numbers that are eaten by predators. The cages need cleaning to remove falling sediment and to ensure that feeding is not disturbed. As the clams grow larger, they are released into the wild to enhance natural clam populations.

Why we must take action for sustainability

As more and more of Earth's wild fish stocks are becoming depleted, it is vital that we put sustainable fishing methods into action. This is especially true considering the great importance of fish as the major protein source for a sixth of the world's population and as a valuable food for even more people the world over. The fast-growing marine aquaculture industry also has a poor sustainability record at the present time in most countries. However, if we can achieve sustainability in both wild and farmed fisheries, then fish could be an even more valuable supply of protein as the world's population increases.

Actions to stop or drastically reduce pollution from land-based and marine sources and dumping at sea are very important to ensure that we have healthy coastal wetlands and waters. Pollution has been so great in many areas that increasing numbers of dead zones are being created where there is no longer any sea life. Toxic chemicals and litter are now found in the most remote places on the planet. We have the technical knowledge to stop some pollution now and to develop new ways of preventing pollution in the future.

Reducing the impact of climate change is another great challenge. Unless we take action to drastically cut the carbon dioxide we produce soon, the Intergovernmental Panel on Climate Change predicts that sea levels could rise as much as 27 inches (69 cm) by 2080. Coastal areas around the planet would be seriously threatened. Of the 15 largest cities in the world, 13 lie on coastal plains, including Shanghai in China and Jakarta in Indonesia. Extreme weather events such as typhoons and cyclones would occur with increasing frequency, causing destruction to coastal communities and environments and low-lying islands.

There is now evidence that marine protected areas allow the production of young fish that restock fishing grounds, provide a safe place for vulnerable species, and help seas to recover from human and natural disturbances.

The brant is a small, dark goose that breeds in the high Arctic. Salt marshes and estuaries on the coasts of North America, China, Japan, and western Europe are valuable winter habitats for this bird. If these habitats are destroyed, it will have a serious impact on the goose population.

The Blackwater estuary in Essex, England, is the site of Abbots Hall Farm. The creation of a salt marsh here will not only help prevent flooding from rising sea levels, but will also bring real benefits for the estuary and its wildlife. Wigeon ducks, shorebirds, and sea lavender will also thrive on the new coastal wetland.

Case Study: Creating natural defenses against rising sea levels at Abbots Hall Farm

The Abbots Hall Farm project in Essex, England, shows that the best defense against rising sea levels caused by climate change is to allow a natural coastline to grow and adapt. This is sometimes known as coastal realignment, and the Abbots Hall project is the largest of its kind ever undertaken in Europe. The farm is situated on the Blackwater estuary, an internationally important area for wildlife.

The project is converting more than a third of a square mile (.84 sq km) of farmland into salt marsh and grassland. The coastal farm aims to show how the re-creation of salt marshes can act as a cost-effective, sustainable sea defense by significantly reducing the impact of waves and protecting the coast from erosion. At the same time, the salt marshes are supporting a rich variety of wildlife.

Salt marshes are frequently lost to make way for tourist developments and the construction of ports and oil terminals. Around two-fifths of a square mile (1 sq km) of salt marsh is lost in southern and eastern England every year, with a global loss of 40 to 50 percent predicted for the next century.

The Abbots Hall Farm project is part of a nationwide initiative to restore the UK's rapidly declining coastal wetlands. Similar projects are taking place in Germany, Scotland, and the U.S.

CHAPTER 7

How you can help keep seas healthy

Taking action for the sustainable use of the seas worldwide is becoming increasingly urgent in the 21st century. We can all help to keep our seas healthy by making simple changes in our lives and reducing our impact on the planet.

When shopping, look for fish and other seafoods that display the Marine Stewardship Council logo (see page 33), which proves they come from sustainable sources.

Cut down your family's use of toxic chemicals to help reduce marine pollution. You can do this by buying organic fruits and vegetables, not using pesticides in your garden, and using environmentally friendly cleaning products in your home. Your school can do the same.

You can help to reduce climate change and its impact on the seas and marine life by reducing the carbon dioxide you produce. Transportation and energy are the two largest sources of this greenhouse gas. Walk, bike, or use public transportation rather than going by car whenever possible. If you travel by car, try to carpool. Save energy by switching off lights and electrical appliances when not in use. Persuade your family to choose energy-efficient lighting and electrical goods. Encourage them to turn down the thermostat on your indoor heating system. Turning it down by 18 °F (10 °C) can save up to 10 percent on your heating bill and benefit the planet as well!

Many forms of man-made litter can take several years to decompose and be a serious threat to marine life. Taking part in a litter cleanup can be a good way to help keep beaches and seas clean.

Underwater diving and snorkeling open up
a wonderful world of marine life, with fish,
anemones, corals, and other animals of a
fantastic range of colors, shapes, and sizes.

Reduce the amount of waste polluting
the oceans by reusing and recycling as
much as possible.

When planning a vacation, go with a tour
operator that is certified as environmentally
responsible. While on vacation, don't leave
litter on beaches. Be careful when you choose
a vacation souvenir, as many corals and
conch shells are threatened because they are
killed for souvenirs.

Don't be tempted to touch wildlife and
disturb habitats on the coast or if you are
diving or snorkeling, and remember that
coral reefs are particularly sensitive. If you
take a whale or dolphin boat trip, make sure
it follows a whale and dolphin watching code

of conduct (see page 38). If you are boating
or jet-skiing, be careful not to disturb
wildlife, and don't keep the engine running
longer than you have to, as this creates noise
and chemical pollution.

You could also get involved by joining WWF
or a marine conservation organization, or by
raising money for marine conservation.
Taking part in an "adopt a whale or dolphin"
program is a way to help conserve cetaceans.
You can find out more from WWF or the
Whale and Dolphin Conservation Society.

Find out more about the amazing life of the
seas, and keep informed about threats and
conservation action by using the Internet
and reading newspapers and books.

Glossary

aquaculture farming of fish and other sea life

biodiversity the whole range of variation in living things—the variety of life

biome a large, naturally occurring community of plants and animals occupying a major habitat; seas and forests are both examples of biomes

commercial done to make money

communities [of plants and animals] groups of living things belonging to different species that occur together in an area and interact

consumer [of plants and animals] a living thing that feeds on other living things

decomposer a living thing that feeds by breaking down dead plants and animals

deforestation the cutting down or destruction of forests

detritus waste matter

diversity variety

economy the supply of money to a community or country from goods and services; the economy of a community that relies on fishing for its main source of income will be badly affected if fish stocks run out

ecosystem all of the plants and animals in an area, along with their environment

estuary the place where a river meets the sea

fertilizer a chemical or natural substance spread and mixed with soil to make it more fertile and to encourage plant growth

fishery a fishing ground, or a place where fish are caught

food chain a series of plants and animals that are each dependent on the next as a source of food

food web all of the food chains that are connected in an ecosystem

fossil fuel a substance such as coal, oil, or gas that is formed from the decomposition of animal and plant remains

genetic relating to something that is passed down from one generation to another within a species

global warming the gradual rise in temperatu over all of Earth's surface

habitat the place where a plant or animal liv

livelihood a way of getting things that are needed for life, such as food and shelter; usually, livelihoods provide money through a job or the trade of goods and services

mammal a warm-blooded animal that feeds its young on milk from its body

migrate to move seasonally, usually over a lo distance, from one habitat or climate to anoth

native [of a species] one that occurs naturally in an area

nutrient a substance that provides nourishme

overfishing taking too many fish

pesticide a substance that kills pests; usually used by farmers to stop crops from being eater

plankton microscopic plants and animals tha float in the sea or fresh water; larger animals as fish feed on plankton

pollutant a substance that causes pollution

pollution presence of high levels of harmful substances in the environment, often as a res of human activity

predator an animal that hunts or kills anothe animal for food

prey an animal that is hunted or killed by another animal for food

producer a living thing that makes food

resource stock or supply of materials or other useful or valuable things; natural resources include the seas and all that they provide

seamount an underwater mountain

sediment matter that settles to the bottom of a liquid; sediments are found on the seabed

species a particular type of living thing

toxic poisonous

wetlands lands made up of marshes or swamp

Further information

Web sites

WWF International
www.panda.org

WWF is an international charity that takes action to protect species and address threats to the environment for the benefit of people and nature. It works for sustainable development. WWF runs "Adopt a Dolphin" and "Adopt a Whale" programs.

Whale and Dolphin Conservation Society
www.wdcs.org

An international charity that works in more than 20 countries for the conservation of whales, dolphins, and their environment. The WDCS also runs an "Adopt a Whale" program.

Marine Mammal Center
www.tmmc.org

This Web site has useful facts on marine mammals, threats, and conservation.

The Ocean Conservancy
www.oceanconservancy.org

A U.S.-based organization, the Ocean Conservancy promotes healthy and diverse ocean ecosystems and opposes practices that threaten ocean life and human life.

Marine Biology
www.marinebio.com

Marine Biology is committed to the conservation of the oceans and marine life.

Marine Stewardship Council
www.msc.org

The Marine Stewardship Council promotes responsible fishing practices around the world.

Books

Dipper, Frances. *Guide to the Oceans*. New York: Dorling Kindersley, 2002.

Frahm, Randy. *Oceans: Lifeblood of the Earth*. Mankato, Minn.: Creative Education, 2001.

Goldman, Linda. *Cleaning Up Our Water*. Chicago: Children's Press, 1994.

Grant, Pamela. *Water: How We Use and Abuse Our Planet*. Mankato, Minn.: Thameside Press, 2000.

Haugen, Hayley Mitchell. *Life in a Coral Reef*. San Diego: Kidhaven Press, 2003.

Hirschi, Ron. *Save Our Oceans and Coasts*. New York: Delacorte Press, 1993.

Hoff, Mary King. *Our Endangered Planet: Oceans*. Minneapolis: Lerner Publications, 1991.

Johnson, Rebecca. *A Journey into the Ocean*. Minneapolis: Carolrhoda Books, 2004.

MacQuitty, Miranda. *Ocean*. New York: Dorling Kindersley, 2004.

Powell, Jillian. *Oil Spills*. Mankato, Minn.: Bridgestone Books, 2003.

Stefanow, Jennifer. *Polluted Waters*. Chicago: Raintree, 2004.

Index